AF731034

Real Estate Riches

Taking the First Step to Buying Your Own Home and Building True Wealth

Brian D'Amico

Real Estate Riches

Printed by:
90-Minute Books
302 Martinique Drive
Winter Haven, FL 33884
www.90minutebooks.com

Copyright © 2018, Brian D'Amico

Published in the United States of America

170922-00913-2

ISBN-13: 978-1643200132
ISBN-10: 1643200135

No parts of this publication may be reproduced without correct attribution to the author of this book.

For more information on 90-Minute Books including finding out how you can publish your own book, visit 90minutebooks.com or call (863) 318-0464

Here's What's Inside...

Introduction

Real Estate Riches!

I come from a real estate family, and I was fortunate enough to buy a home when I first got out of college. I've been able to take that first home (two-family) and leverage it many times to set myself up with more investments over the course of my lifetime.

I wrote this book because I wanted to share my years of success and failures. I realize that when I first started, I couldn't have been greener. I wish there had been a book out there like this, which had offered a simple yet effective blueprint explaining what to look for and help with my strategy.

It saddens me that a lot of people are renting because of the massive recession we had in 2008. These people are sitting out of an industry that can be very lucrative and help them build a life for them and their family.

Rent has never been tax-deductible, and their rental payments many times over would be the same as owning a home today! Remember that mortgage interest and real estate taxes are tax-deductible.

In this book you will understand what it takes to get started in real estate. The wisdom within will help you with your planning process and goal setting, which is a key part of real estate investing.

Enjoy the book!

I hope this book educates you on not just buying your first home but on creating wealth in the real estate industry and inspires you to get started today!

To Your Success!

Brian D'Amico

P.S. You may be thinking, can this little book really teach me everything I need to know about real estate investing? The truth is, this book could have very well been 200 pages, but I want to make sure you get professional advice as things change rapidly when it comes to real estate and finance. Think of this book as a 2000-foot view, looking down on strategy as a whole.

Take Care of Your Living Situation First and Buy Your First Home

Let's face it: To win a jackpot, you have to play the game. To win the lottery, you have to buy a ticket. If you want to be a successful real-estate investor, you have to be IN the real-estate industry. The first step should be buying your own home. You might be single or have a family, but no matter your situation, real estate doesn't differ. You just might need a larger home with more bedrooms.

If you currently don't own a home, I'd like to share a simple but effective strategy that will get you on the right track—drum roll, please!

Buy a Multi Family. When I say "multi family," this could be a 2-unit, 3-unit, or even 4-unit building. Now many people who are just starting out might favor a single-family house or condo, but the truth of the matter is, if you know you want to follow a path of real estate success, BUY A MULTI as your first home.

There are many reasons for this; here are a few that will get your mind racing:

(1) You have somebody else helping you pay your mortgage. Depending on your area and rental comps, often the other unit(s) will pay a large portion of your mortgage, which always helps.

(2) You can be approved for more when applying for a mortgage. TIP: You can count 75% of the rental income towards your income, which will help in obtaining a larger mortgage.

(3) You get to practice being a landlord. What better place to practice than the home that you live in? You will start to understand things that could go wrong. You will also start to build your team of people in the trades. For example, you will soon learn that you will need a plumber, electrician, handyman, landscaper, driveway repairer, HVAC installer, Flooring installer, snow remover, etc.

If you can't afford to hire tradesmen when you first start out, that's okay. Instead, you have an opportunity to become a jack-of-all-trades, addressing issues in all areas of your home yourself. Think of these skills as a first-step in your move to becoming a real-estate investor. Everything you're learning will help you with renovating investment properties in the future.

(4) You can keep your first home when you move into a new home. If you bought your multi correctly and have built equity through the years, and you know it will be cash flow-positive when you move out,

there is no reason to sell. Yes, it might be easier just to sell the asset to move into a new home, but why, if it's making money? If you need to raise funds for the down payment, you can always take an equity line and use the funds any way you see fit. Again, it might not be easier, but like we say on our podcast "Easy Money New England," there is no such thing as easy money!

Here are some basic steps to follow when looking to buy your first multi-family:

(1) Meet up with a loan officer. My company, New Fed Mortgage Corp., has many loan officers who are great at their craft. When you go over your goals and objectives, you may say, "I want to buy a two-family home. These are the cities I'm looking in. This seems to be the price range. Do I qualify?"

We can help you answer those questions. The loan officer will be able to tell you what the proposed interest rate and payment would be after running a credit report. They'll review the real estate taxes and homeowner's insurance when you are looking at a specific address, so you know all expenses of that property up front.

(2) A good loan officer will have a great network of real estate agents and will be able to get you answers in the city in which you are looking. realtors will be

able to supply comparable sales in the area and give you data on how the rental units are priced. We suggest meeting the real estate agent, especially if they have some properties to show you. It may take you a little bit of time to find that perfect place, but take your time, and you will find it. Obviously, you are going to be living there and you want to like your living arrangement. The good news is, if you're looking to buy your first home, there are a lot of good first-time home buyer programs. You don't need 20% down to buy your first home. A common misconception is that you need 20% down to buy your home. You can get into your first home with as little as 3% down.

Some programs allow you to buy a home with no money down. If the property is in a rural area and it's considered USDA-approved, you can get a home with no money down! The same is true if you're a veteran. You can get a home with no money down. Obviously, there are qualifiers. You must have a job, or you must have enough income to qualify. If neither of these options applies to you, there are also many down-payment assistance programs available today.

(3) Meet up with your attorney. You may know a great attorney, but they may not specialize in real estate law. Loan officers

and realtors know the best real estate attorneys and they can be instrumental in making you successful. Many buyers never meet their attorneys until the closing date, but it's like anything else; build that relationship and attorneys can be your best ally for structuring offers and purchase and sales agreements.

When your mortgage people and real estate people and attorneys work well together, and they do this regularly, you want to tap into that.

Wherever you shop for a home, there are experts in those cities, especially when it comes to realtors and attorneys.

You want to invest in cities you know. You want to know things about how that city works. Where you currently live might not be the right city because there might not be a lot of multi-families. So, you might invest in a different city. You still want to understand that city and do your research. What are the demographics? Is it a city where there are a lot of people renting? Is there a local college, and if so, is there student housing?

You want to make sure you are investing in a city that people want to live in, and which has a robust rental market.

Not a Get-Rich-Quick Scheme

Real estate creates more millionaires in this country than any other industry. When you hear families that have major wealth or major income, a large majority of the time, when you look closer, it came from real estate. I believe real estate is the best investment class out there; I believe it's better than stocks, mutual funds, crypto currencies, or precious metals. Real estate is the best investment you can ever make.

It's not a get-rich-quick scheme, though. You must plan for the long game. Unfortunately, when I was younger, I didn't understand this fully. Real estate investing seemed like a very slow and dull profession. Looking back on it, I sold many properties as a real estate sales agent instead of buying these properties myself. The truth is, I couldn't stand the downtime and needed to have more action. I had great opportunities to buy many more properties, but I didn't understand that real estate is just another investment class. Being younger, I preferred investing in stocks, primarily because it's an asset class you don't have to work on. There is no such thing as tenant calls about no heat, frozen pipes, doorbell not working, or stove not working—and no such thing as tenants not paying the rent!

What I didn't realize is I could have been investing all along, and had a management company to take care of these issues for me. For example, many property management companies charge 10% of the total income on your building(s). I know of one investor who gives 15% if his phone doesn't ring at all during the month. That seems very fair to me and a great incentive. TIP: Not all management companies are EQUAL. I have seen some horror stories and it is extremely important you select the right management company. I have seen managers who steal from their landlords and it can be easy to hide costs and price up invoices, so buyer BEWARE.

This strategy is called "Buy and Hold," and we will talk about this in a little more depth in the next few chapters. Many people try to go quicker and do "Fix and Flips," which we will also talk about.

In any event, I encourage you to dream big in this space. Think about what kind of income you'd love to have from real estate, and then reverse engineer your plan and design a strategy that fits your lifestyle goals.

For example: If your goal is to make $10,000 a month, to replace your day job, you can build a plan to create that. It won't happen overnight, but if you work on getting your team together it can happen much more quickly than if you try to do it yourself. Your team should consist of a real estate attorney, a loan officer, a real estate agent and depending whether or not you will manage yourself, a property manager. Eventually you will also need a solid accountant.

Another great thing about this business is once you get the first one under your belt, the others become easier. The business can be difficult to grow when you first start out, but eventually you get to know the people who can help you realize your dream. Remember, if you are successful, your team is successful too.

The first step to get a full understanding of where you are and where you want to go is to talk with a loan officer. My company New Fed Mortgage was established in 2000 and we are here to help people achieve their goals. Our mission statement is "We strive to improve peoples' lives." We can always be reached at 1-877-New-FED-1 to let us know you want to get started!

Flip or Flop

A book on real estate investing wouldn't be complete without sharing the good along with the bad. No matter what you do, there's no such thing as easy money. You must work at it. Although I've been successful in real estate, I have had my fair share of setbacks. In the interest of sharing what not to do, let me share with you the story of when I tried to cash out and make a quick buck in this industry.

We've all heard of "Fix and Flips," right? Well, this is my story of a "Fix and Flop." Looking back, I truly didn't have the time to get involved as much as I needed to make it a success. I had a young family and a full-time job, so I relied on others. I felt like they knew what they were doing, so I just sat back and figured it would all work out. They missed all their timeframes. Anything that could have gone wrong went wrong. We didn't pay attention to the home inspection as much as we probably should have.

Unless you can invest a lot of time, like full time, I wouldn't dabble in it. You must be hands-on. You must know every area of the house. Just because you bought the house, you're not going to put some paint on it and sell it. You might have some plumbing issues. You might have some roofing issues. You might have to redo the landscaping. All these things cost money, and they always cost more money than you project, especially if you must pay others to do the work.

The other thing that costs money is borrowing costs. This is where things started to go off the rails for us. If you must take a big mortgage out and you're thinking you're going to sell that house in, say, four months, but you don't sell it for more like a year or year and a half, you just lost a lot of money due to carrying costs. Even though it's tax deductible, check with your accountant because investment property tax law changes. If you were expecting to sell the house in four months and it took you a year and a half, well, you're going to lose every time. There's something wrong with this equation.

Because things took longer than expected on the flip and we missed all our timeframes, we missed the fall market and went into the winter. We then had to winterize the property. No one was looking at properties in the northeast at the time. On top of that, it wasn't priced right, and as painful as it is to admit now, we paid too much for the property considering all that was wrong with it. Although we lost money on the deal and it was a flop, I didn't lose the lesson. Have you heard of "fail forward?" This was an expensive lesson, but if I were ever to get involved in another project like this again, I will know the pitfalls and things to watch out for. Remember, I'm trying to share my failures as much as I can so the new investor can understand the pitfalls before they get started.

Buy and Hold

A long time ago, I had a friend in the industry who amassed enormous amounts of property in very good locations. He says that a lot of the "flip people" are playing checkers, but that using a buy-and-hold strategy is playing chess. He's building for the long-term, and these guys are focused on the short term.

Everyone wants to make money. Everyone wants to do it as quickly as possible. The name of the game in real estate is *cash flow*. When you increase your cash flow, that's a buy-and-hold strategy. If I buy a house for $100,000 and I sell it for $150,000, well great, I made $50,000. That's excellent, right? But I must pay capital gains on that money, so there are some taxes involved, and I have no income coming in after that sale. I'm not building anything. I'm just going for the quick turnaround money, and I must do another one and keep doing the work over and over again to become successful. It works for some people, but at the end of the day, you don't have long-term equity or more importantly CASH FLOW.

With a buy-and-hold strategy, you still have expenses on that property, but the tenants that pay rent will make it cash flow-positive. So, if your first property is positive, you want to duplicate your efforts and get into your second property that's cash flow-positive as well. Financing-wise you are probably taking out 30-

year mortgages, but if you can do a 15-year mortgage, that's even better because of the decreased interest you will pay over the years.

I come from the school of making the lowest payment you can on a fixed mortgage, because you can always pay it down. And when you start paying it down, that's when you get into the time savings of that 30-year amortization, which we will discuss further in the next chapter. Also by going to the full term of a 30-year mortgage you are increasing your cash flow because the monthly mortgage payment will be much lower.

TIP: Residential property is considered from one unit to four units. If the property has five or more units it is considered commercial property and commercial loan terms will be different than your typical residential mortgage. It will most likely require a 20-year amortization schedule that will need to be refinanced or extended every five years.

How to Tap into Your Equity and Create Wealth

If you look at a typical 30-year fixed mortgage, say it's a $200,000 mortgage, in the first five years you're not paying off much principal. You'll see that, at the end of five years, you've paid very little principal.

Year	Pmt Date	Rate	Payment	Principal	Interest	MI	Balance
1	09/27/2018	4.250	11,806.56	3,371.72	8,434.84	0.00	196,628.28
2	09/27/2019	4.250	11,806.56	3,517.86	8,288.70	0.00	193,110.42
3	09/27/2020	4.250	11,806.56	3,670.32	8,136.24	0.00	189,440.10
4	09/27/2021	4.250	11,806.56	3,829.38	7,977.18	0.00	185,610.72
5	09/27/2022	4.250	11,806.56	3,995.35	7,811.21	0.00	181,615.37
6	09/27/2023	4.250	11,806.56	4,168.48	7,638.08	0.00	177,446.89
7	09/27/2024	4.250	11,806.56	4,349.12	7,457.44	0.00	173,097.77
8	09/27/2025	4.250	11,806.56	4,537.63	7,268.93	0.00	168,560.14
9	09/27/2026	4.250	11,806.56	4,734.28	7,072.28	0.00	163,825.86
10	09/27/2027	4.250	11,806.56	4,939.43	6,867.13	0.00	158,886.43
11	09/27/2028	4.250	11,806.56	5,153.52	6,653.04	0.00	153,732.91
12	09/27/2029	4.250	11,806.56	5,376.85	6,429.71	0.00	148,356.06
13	09/27/2030	4.250	11,806.56	5,609.86	6,196.70	0.00	142,746.20
14	09/27/2031	4.250	11,806.56	5,852.97	5,953.59	0.00	136,893.23
15	09/27/2032	4.250	11,806.56	6,106.64	5,699.92	0.00	130,786.59
16	09/27/2033	4.250	11,806.56	6,371.27	5,435.29	0.00	124,415.32
17	09/27/2034	4.250	11,806.56	6,647.41	5,159.15	0.00	117,767.91
18	09/27/2035	4.250	11,806.56	6,935.49	4,871.07	0.00	110,832.42
19	09/27/2036	4.250	11,806.56	7,236.05	4,570.51	0.00	103,596.37
20	09/27/2037	4.250	11,806.56	7,549.64	4,256.92	0.00	96,046.73
21	09/27/2038	4.250	11,806.56	7,876.82	3,929.74	0.00	88,169.91
22	09/27/2039	4.250	11,806.56	8,218.19	3,588.37	0.00	79,951.72
23	09/27/2040	4.250	11,806.56	8,574.36	3,232.20	0.00	71,377.36
24	09/27/2041	4.250	11,806.56	8,945.94	2,860.62	0.00	62,431.42
25	09/27/2042	4.250	11,806.56	9,333.64	2,472.92	0.00	53,097.78
26	09/27/2043	4.250	11,806.56	9,738.14	2,068.42	0.00	43,359.64
27	09/27/2044	4.250	11,806.56	10,160.17	1,646.39	0.00	33,199.47
28	09/27/2045	4.250	11,806.56	10,600.51	1,206.05	0.00	22,598.96
29	09/27/2046	4.250	11,806.56	11,059.88	746.68	0.00	11,539.08
30	09/27/2047	4.250	11,806.45	11,539.08	267.37	0.00	0.00

Diagram: After five years of paying $983.88 for principal and interest, after making 60 payments you still have a balance of $181,615.

You might be saying to yourself that you know this, and it doesn't help much, but now I want to give you a few strategies to start creating more equity in your newly acquired home.

The first strategy is very simple, and it's to make a lump sum principal payment on your mortgage.

Pmt#	Pmt Date	Rate	Payment	Principal	Interest	MI	Balance
1	10/27/2017	4.250	983.88	275.55	708.33	0.00	199,724.45
2	11/27/2017	4.250	983.88	276.52	707.36	0.00	199,447.93
3	12/27/2017	4.250	983.88	277.50	706.38	0.00	199,170.43
4	01/27/2018	4.250	983.88	278.48	705.40	0.00	198,891.95
5	02/27/2018	4.250	983.88	279.47	704.41	0.00	198,612.48
6	03/27/2018	4.250	983.88	280.46	703.42	0.00	198,332.02
7	04/27/2018	4.250	983.88	281.45	702.43	0.00	198,050.57
8	05/27/2018	4.250	983.88	282.45	701.43	0.00	197,768.12
9	06/27/2018	4.250	983.88	283.45	700.43	0.00	197,484.67
10	07/27/2018	4.250	983.88	284.46	699.42	0.00	197,200.21
11	08/27/2018	4.250	983.88	285.46	698.42	0.00	196,914.75
12	09/27/2018	4.250	983.88	286.47	697.41	0.00	196,628.28
13	10/27/2018	4.250	983.88	287.49	696.39	0.00	196,340.79
14	11/27/2018	4.250	983.88	288.51	695.37	0.00	196,052.28
15	12/27/2018	4.250	983.88	289.53	694.35	0.00	195,762.75
16	01/27/2019	4.250	983.88	290.55	693.33	0.00	195,472.20
17	02/27/2019	4.250	983.88	291.58	692.30	0.00	195,180.62
18	03/27/2019	4.250	983.88	292.62	691.26	0.00	194,888.00
19	04/27/2019	4.250	983.88	293.65	690.23	0.00	194,594.35
20	05/27/2019	4.250	983.88	294.69	689.19	0.00	194,299.66
21	06/27/2019	4.250	983.88	295.74	688.14	0.00	194,003.92
22	07/27/2019	4.250	983.88	296.78	687.10	0.00	193,707.14
23	08/27/2019	4.250	983.88	297.83	686.05	0.00	193,409.31
24	09/27/2019	4.250	983.88	298.89	684.99	0.00	193,110.42
25	10/27/2019	4.250	983.88	299.95	683.93	0.00	192,810.47
26	11/27/2019	4.250	983.88	301.01	682.87	0.00	192,509.46
27	12/27/2019	4.250	983.88	302.08	681.80	0.00	192,207.38
28	01/27/2020	4.250	983.88	303.15	680.73	0.00	191,904.23
29	02/27/2020	4.250	983.88	304.22	679.66	0.00	191,600.01
30	03/27/2020	4.250	983.88	305.30	678.58	0.00	191,294.71
31	04/27/2020	4.250	983.88	306.38	677.50	0.00	190,988.33
32	05/27/2020	4.250	983.88	307.46	676.42	0.00	190,680.87
33	06/27/2020	4.250	983.88	308.55	675.33	0.00	190,372.32
34	07/27/2020	4.250	983.88	309.64	674.24	0.00	190,062.68
35	08/27/2020	4.250	983.88	310.74	673.14	0.00	189,751.94
36	09/27/2020	4.250	983.88	311.84	672.04	0.00	189,440.10
37	10/27/2020	4.250	983.88	312.95	670.93	0.00	189,127.15
38	11/27/2020	4.250	983.88	314.05	669.83	0.00	188,813.10
39	12/27/2020	4.250	983.88	315.17	668.71	0.00	188,497.93
40	01/27/2021	4.250	983.88	316.28	667.60	0.00	188,181.65
41	02/27/2021	4.250	983.88	317.40	666.48	0.00	187,864.25
42	03/27/2021	4.250	983.88	318.53	665.35	0.00	187,545.72
43	04/27/2021	4.250	983.88	319.66	664.22	0.00	187,226.06
44	05/27/2021	4.250	983.88	320.79	663.09	0.00	186,905.27
45	06/27/2021	4.250	983.88	321.92	661.96	0.00	186,583.35
46	07/27/2021	4.250	983.88	323.06	660.82	0.00	186,260.29
47	08/27/2021	4.250	983.88	324.21	659.67	0.00	185,936.08
48	09/27/2021	4.250	983.88	325.36	658.52	0.00	185,610.72

Diagram: You will see in your first payment only $275.55 would go towards your principal. The best scenario I can see—if you made an extra principal payment of $550.00, you just shortened your term by two payments (or 2 months).

If you were to pay $5,000 towards your principal, you're actually buying time and decreasing the term of the loan. You have now prepaid your principal over the course of 17 months! Your 30-year mortgage just became 28 years and 7 months remaining.

First year = $3,372 then the following months of principal payments = $287.49, $288.51, $289.53, $290.55, $291.58, $292.62 – By following this example you are quickly learning how the banks compute interest and you are shortening your term without refinancing or changing any terms of your loan.

Important Note:

Looking at this schedule, you will see that at the end of this 30-year term you have paid $354,196.80 on a $200,000 loan.

This is 77% more than the initial balance!

This is a simple strategy that I used for many years, but I was very frugal and was very regimented when it came to budgeting.

Remember, your terms are not going to change just because you're paying down the mortgage. Your interest rate doesn't change, your payment doesn't change. But when you make that extra principal payment, you're paying down the amortization schedule to truly shorten that term.

I advise you to keep good records when following this strategy because banks and/or servicers make mistakes. I always kept my amortization schedule handy and it became a game of how many payments I could eliminate as I followed the system.

I know many people might not have extra money hanging around—that would lead to another strategy that takes a bit to learn—but it has saved me a tremendous amount of savings over the last few years. You wouldn't need any additional money.

This strategy is called a **Mortgage Acceleration** program and you can develop your plan if (1) you have equity in your home, (2) you make more money than you spend, and (3) you have a credit score of at least 660.

The basics of this program are that you obtain a home equity line of credit, pay your mortgage principal balance down monthly, and then replenish the equity line when your income comes in during the month. Simply put, you are using your checking account balance to pay down your mortgage and replenishing it through your equity line to pay off all your bills. The reason this works is derived from one key banking principle: **Interest on your mortgage is calculated on the daily balance.**

Make no mistake about this program, it is life-changing and I can't say enough good things about it. I am a little embarrassed that I couldn't figure it out the first time I saw this back in 2008. I really grasped the technique only after a one-on-one coaching call with the mortgage acceleration coach Harj Gill, who is the godfather of this system, and who was responsible for bringing this to Australia, where it swept the country.

I have seen some great results from many people and I believe my 30-year mortgage will be paid off in less than five years. The system I have used can be found on my website www.briandamico.com and I highly recommend getting the one-on-one coaching session. The system has a software component that will keep you on track so that you are not enslaved to your 30-year mortgage. All people are different, but this is a game-changer when it comes to increasing your equity and paying off debts much sooner than your typical borrower. I'd like to add that this is not a scam or illegal. This is very common in Australia where most people in that country follow this system, which might be why Australia is known to be the happiest country!

OK so now you're asking, "Why do I want to pay down the mortgage more quickly?"

(1) It is going to create equity in that home for you. When the time comes for you to buy another investment property and you need to come up with another down payment of 20%, this gives you the

opportunity to take an equity line. Use that money to buy your next property, rinse, and repeat! If you look at people who have built wealth in real estate, they almost always use their equity position in one home to buy their next one. It's a really good strategy to have an equity line as a second position in your current home and use it to leverage your next property—that increases your CASH FLOW.

(2) You are creating more opportunities within your portfolio to have less leverage which always gives you more buying POWER.

Example: Let's say you want to buy a $300,000 three-family investment property. You need 20% to buy it, so you need $60,000. Most people don't have an extra $60,000 lying around, so you can take that from your equity line. I consider this good debt because the money you're going to make off that three-family property, based on the $60,000, is far more than you'll get if you just keep the equity in your home and not use it!

It's a great strategy for amassing more property. And then, obviously, you're doing it again to increase CASH FLOW.

You're going to have rental income that's going to help you pay all your bills. It's a great strategy to make sure you're leveraging all your assets to make more cash flow. At the end of the day, it's all about cash flow. It doesn't matter what you owe. If you're cash flow-positive every month, that's good debt. Remember, if your debt is making you money, that is ALWAYS good debt!

TIP: When buying real estate, you want to figure out the cap rate. The higher the cap rate the better!

The capitalization rate, often just called the cap rate, is the ratio of Net Operating Income (NOI) to Property Asset Value. So, for example, if a property recently sold for $500,000 and had an NOI of $50,000/yearly, then the cap rate would be $50,000/$500,000, or 10%.

Professionals purchasing commercial properties, for example, may buy at a 4% cap rate in high-demand areas, or a 10% (or even higher) cap rate in low-demand areas. Generally, 4% to 10% per year is a reasonable range for your investment property to earn.

Finding Your First Investment Property Deal

Ideally, you would already own your first house. Depending on how long you've lived in it, it may take you a little bit to build up some equity. Ideally, you want 20%–25% to put down on an investment property, depending on where you are getting your mortgage. When you make that 20% down payment, depending on what the purchase price is, you want to figure out which city you want to invest in.

I could tell you many stories of people who were very successful when they invested in the areas they lived in, or they invested in the areas they know. As soon as they went outside of the territory, that's when problems began, because they didn't know the market. On one of the flips I did, I didn't know my market, and that's why I lost. It was a market I thought I knew but didn't. So, you want to invest in a market you know.

If it's in a city where you own your first property, that's the area you know. Or maybe it's close to a major city. For a rental, you want to make sure that the property is cash flow-positive and you want to start doing numbers with your loan officer and real estate agent. What can you expect for rent based on bedroom count? Once you figure out bedroom count and rent, that will obviously help dictate what city you want to invest in.

By this time, it might be three, four, five years after you bought your first house that you were able to build a little bit of equity. Or maybe you got lucky, and the values were on the rise when you bought. Maybe five years down the road, with the increased equity in your home and the little bit you've been doing to pay it down, if there's an equity position there, you can get a second lien on your home as an equity line. You only pay what you use, and you have the ability to get that down payment if you haven't been able to save it through your typical checking or savings accounts.

You want to determine the city you want to start in. If you're going to buy more than one property, you'd like to focus in and around an area. If you're going to manage some properties, you want to make sure they're close. You want to make sure it's easy to collect the rent. All of these things go into your decision-making process. Some people do things over state lines and have been successful, but you would need a property management company—it can be done! I know of a few investors that primarily invest in properties in Memphis, TN and Tampa Bay, FL. You can look up recent podcasts at briandamico.com. We bring you all kinds of successful real estate investors and bring money-making opportunities to our podcast on a weekly basis!

Once you figure out where you want to go, you just need to figure out what your mortgage payment would be on, say 20% down on a three-family, or 25% down, depending on property type. Get with a loan officer and have them run the numbers for you.

If you could make $1,500 a month by owning a piece of property and be cash flow-positive, I don't think there's anything wrong with that. In fact, in some cities you can make much more than that. When rates are low, that's when you see house values rise because of the affordability factor. Obviously, you can afford more because the rates are keeping your payment lower. When rates are higher, home values go lower. There is a relationship between interest rates and home prices and affordability.

TIP: Keeping track of the 10-year bond yield price is always the closest indicator to mortgage rates. If you wanted to keep track of this index on your phone, you will be able to gauge where rates are going; the higher the yield the higher the rates: SYMBOL =^TNX.

Once you have your first investment property under your belt, you have more options going forward. You could sell that property and trade the proceeds using something called a 1031 exchange.

What Is a 1031 Exchange?

Once you have your first investment property under your belt, you have more options going forward. Success creates options!

The IRS definition of a 1031 exchange:

Under Section 1031 of the United States Internal Revenue Code (26 U.S.C. § 1031), a taxpayer may defer recognition of capital gains and related Federal income tax liability on the exchange of certain types of property.

Let me show you how it works. Let's say you have a three-family property you bought five years ago for $300,000.

It's now worth $450,000. You had a little bit of luck there, but it's cash flow-positive. There's a strategy in which you sell that property and take all the proceeds and invest them into another three-family, or even a six-family or a nine-family. If you use a 1031 exchange, you don't have to pay taxes on that gain you made. It's tax-deferred. You're deferring that tax, and by doing so you are increasing your cash flow because you are trading for something with increased cash flow (more units)!

One of my mentors in this space used to teach this strategy to all of his investors. He called it "The yellow brick road to success." It was simple to follow because it was a platform to increase your cash flow anytime you had a chance. It worked very well for my mentor because he had people selling many large buildings through him and he would also get the new buildings they were buying. Looking back on it, it was genius. I remember working late nights and calculating the cap rates on all commercial buildings that were on the market. I remember finding a few around 12%–14% and investors were very interested.

I have seen one buyer start off with one 3-family building and continually use the 1031 exchange to trade up. The last I saw he traded up to a 36-unit building. Talk about increased cash flow!! Remember, these are not sophisticated strategies, just a little reading up and having a good team in place. You would look for a qualified intermediary (QI) who would hold your funds in escrow, which again can be searched on one of my podcasts on www.briandamico.com. It's important to select the right QI.

Good Debt versus Bad Debt: It's All about Cash Flow

Say you buy a car—it's a beautiful car—and you love it. But you paid $60,000 for it. Unless you're renting it out, that's bad debt. If you're going to take debt out and it's going to make you positive cash flow, that's good debt. So, a car is bad debt. If you buy an expensive watch or this or that, that's all bad debt because it's not getting you anywhere. Good debt is that six-unit building you just bought; yes, you have a lot of debt on that building, but you're making money every month because of that debt. That's good debt.

When I was younger, I read a lot of books such as *Rich Dad, Poor Dad* and always had some sort of mentor (some bad, some good), but it took me a long time to understand that everything you do is hard work and *there are no shortcuts*. I have been in the mortgage business since 2000, and was in the residential and commercial real estate business for five years before that. And you know, no one's there to lead you in the right direction, so you often feel lost and aren't sure if you're doing things the "right way." I want this book to be a confidence booster that can help you make decisions. I've been learning this industry since 1995, and I'm still learning every day.

So let's find some good debt! If you find a property you may be interested in, you can go to the loan officer and say, "Okay, I have this three-family I want to buy." They will then walk you through the process. If you don't have a property, find a good realtor. I know agents who have created wealth for many of their customers. They are always looking at what's coming on the market and can be a great source of information for you. Again, you can't and shouldn't try to do this alone. Tap into the industry. Build your team.

We know many real estate agents who will lead you to great investment opportunities:

Realtor: "Alright, you want to buy an investment property? Here's a great one for you. Here's the rent roll. And this is what the property makes right now."

You would take that rent roll and you would see the purchase price. You bring that to your loan officer and say, "Can you tell me what it will cost on my mortgage for this property?" When you get the numbers, make sure it's principal, interest, real estate taxes, and insurance. That's your full payment. So, when you figure out what that full payment is versus that rent roll, you want to make sure it is cash flow-positive and the cap rate is reasonable.

You may have other expenses that you want to factor in too, such as managing the property. You may have some common utility bills. You want to make sure that if the property is separately metered, there's no serious work that needs to be done. You want to get a home inspection. Other than that, if you're looking at straight numbers, you'll know what the full payment will be versus what the rent roll is. In an effort to keep this simple, if I have a monthly payment of $3,000, but I'm making $5,000 total income, that's $2,000 net income per month. That is good debt!

TIP: If you want to make a quick rule-of-thumb check on whether the rent roll makes the property a good investment, use the one-percent rule. With the one-percent rule, you calculate 1% of the selling value of the property and use that for your rent baseline. So, with a $250,000 property, the one-percent rule tells you the rent baseline should be $2,500.

If you think you'll be able to raise rent or get the property for a lower purchase price, you can adjust the numbers accordingly and compare. Just remember that the key is to have the mortgage payment and any other expenses (insurance, taxes, maintenance) come in at a lower cost than rent. The difference between those two numbers is your positive cash flow.

Some people think your primary home is a good investment, but is it? Is it bringing in money or losing money every month? I could probably debate this with many people, but good debt simply means you are making money from that debt and not losing. Maybe, these new trends like minimalists and living below your means are on to something. Subscribe to our video podcast to hear shows on all of the new trends. You can find us on iTunes, Podbean, IHeart Radio, YouTube, Facebook, and many other places. It's called "Easy Money New England," where we like to say, "There is no such thing as Easy Money."

Breaking Down Opportunity

How do you go about finding opportunities? Get with a great realtor who will set you up with a system whereby if you know the cities you want to invest in, they'll put you on their MLS search system. Then every day or every week, when a new property comes on the market, you're going to get an email about it.

Ask to get setup on email alerts anytime a property gets sold in that city, so you'll see what the market is calling for price-wise. Data is your friend and will help you know if a property is a good deal or not.

It's very important that you pick the right realtor who will help you find properties. Sometimes they know of deals before they come onto the MLS; you want to be their friend so they think of you first. Once you've done your homework and know what things are selling for, when one becomes available you will want to be able to move quickly. That means you have already been pre-approved by your mortgage company and you have your trusted attorney picked out. Many times, the attorney can run title work for you in advance so you know if it's going to go smoothly or if the property has issues.

Here are a few more ways to find strategies for buying homes:

(1) Talk to Sellers/Realtors – Find out the seller's motivation. Many times they are

willing to hold a first or second mortgage that will aid in coming up with more money. Having the seller hold a private 2nd mortgage is a great strategy.

(2) Short Sale – Many times sellers are looking to sell their homes for less than what they owe, and it will need to be approved by the bank.

(3) Foreclosures – Finding sellers that are in pre-foreclosure can be a great way to find a good deal.

(4) Paying for Real Estate Tax Liens – If the seller doesn't pay their taxes, you are in first lien position and can obtain the property.

(5) For Sale by Owner – Many times sellers try to save money and do it themselves, which is not always successful, but worth looking at.

(6) REO's – These are properties the bank owns. The bank primarily works with a few good realtors to get them sold quickly.

(7) Auctions – I have been to many auctions and occasionally you can get a decent deal. The bank still must be willing to let the house go below market—and sometimes they do.

I'm not going to go into much detail on these strategies, because if you have the right team of professionals they will lead you in the right direction. You might have one realtor that specializes in bank-owned properties, and you might have another that gets great investment-quality buildings. You need to have people constantly looking for you and make sure they know you are a serious buyer.

Anytime you are looking to buy your first home or investment property, simply go to www.newfed.com or call 1-877-New-Fed-1 and mention this book. You can also check out www.briandamico.com for all kinds of tools, forms, and calculators that will help you with all facets of investing.

Goal-Setting Strategies and Keeping Score

Having a goal for your real estate business is critical for success. You can't just wing it. If you don't have a goal, it's like a ship that doesn't have a destination. If you don't know where you're going, you're just going to keep going around and around. If you can pinpoint what you're trying to accomplish, whether it's a certain dollar amount you want to make per month, or a certain number of units you're trying to accomplish, you can get there. You just need a solid plan, and you must understand that it takes time.

Real estate is a slow-moving yet exciting ride that creates wealth for a lot of people who understand that it's a slow game.

If you understand that real estate is slow-moving and just another type of asset class, it's a great, great business. You're building wealth. It does take time, but you're building wealth. You want to set your goals, and reverse-engineer your goals. If you say, "I want to make $10,000 net profit per month," ok, how do you get there? A little bit of simple math and you will see that you would need four buildings making $2500 each per month, or maybe two larger buildings. Whatever you desire, it can happen.

If you already own a home, great! You're ahead of the game. You own your own home, and you know you want to be in the real estate business. You know you want to create passive income. Let's look at your financial picture. Everybody's financial picture is different. This includes how much money you make, how much money you save, what your payments are on your current home, and what kind of equity you have in your home. Everyone has different goals for different reasons.

Being a landlord isn't for everyone. In a way, it's a full-time job. I've seen people make it look easy, but it's not easy. Tenants are calling you for a lot of different things. "No heat" calls, no hot water, a flood in their basement, a squeaky cabinet, the light's not working. It can be overwhelming, especially if you already have a full-time job.

Just like you save for retirement with your 401k, you need to save for real estate. It's not without some risk. Many people are risk-averse. I feel like there is more risk in NOT taking action than in taking action. If you don't start building wealth to support your family, and you're relying on a job, who knows what's going to happen in the future? We might all be replaced by robots!

If you create your own gig, you're self-employed, with your real estate portfolio and your holdings, you're setting yourself up for the future. A lot of people don't plan to fail, but they fail to plan. If you start planning that you're going to add so many units over a course of so many years, just do the math. Whenever you find something that works, you duplicate it—and you duplicate it; and you duplicate it again. Before you know it, you amass some property. These properties typically increase in value, and better yet, generate a positive cash flow.

There are cycles to the real estate market. On a buy-and-hold strategy, when you see the fluctuations in the real estate market, those landlords don't get hurt because their cash flow didn't get affected. Even if their assets fell in value, their rent still stayed the same. You can weather more storms because you have positive cash flow. If there is a downturn in the market, you just keep doing what you're doing. You don't panic. You can use it as an opportunity to buy more property, but you don't panic.

Remember, this is a long-term strategy. You're not speculating on real estate. Leave that for the stock market. When the values drop, the opportunity for you to refinance might go away, but you won't need to refinance if the cash flow is positive. Maybe you have an equity line that's already open, with which you're able to scoop up some properties at lower levels. I never knew what the saying meant that "cash is king" until 2008 reared its ugly head.

TIP: You may want to structure your first investment property under an LLC. Check with your attorney and insurance agent, but you may want to start with an LLC or a trust to purchase real estate. This will help with liability and many accountants and attorneys suggest setting up an LLC for every property owned.

OK, now you own some property and it's time to keep score. This is when you will want to maintain a personal financial statement. Typically, a financial statement should be completed once a year.

Sadly, I was never taught this in school. I'm not going to bash high school or some colleges, but this is not in today's curriculum. There is no financial literacy class, and therefore I'd like to add this diagram on the next page that illustrates a simple way of keeping score. When you look at your financial statements yearly, you will see the increased equity positions every year just from keeping up your mortgage payments. I can assure you that it gets fun, and you start making decisions based on increasing your net worth as you continually try to improve your financial position.

Exhibit A:

Example LLC
Balance Sheet
as Of Jan 1st, 2018

<u>**Assets**</u>

Cash in Banks & Investments

NewFed Bank Checking Account	$7500

Real Estate

137 Main St, Boston, MA (2-unit)	$600,000 (FMV)

<u>**Liabilities**</u>

Mortgage Payable- 137 Main St., Boston, MA	$328,000

<u>**Net Worth**</u>- 100% Brian D'Amico	$279,500

The diagram above shows your assets minus any liabilities. Each entity should be listed individually. If you have three LLC's they should be listed individually with three different exhibits. Your personal name exhibit should list all net worth entities and tally up the total, so you have one net worth number personally. Remember, on your personal page you can list things such as stocks, bonds, mutual funds, retirement accounts, and cash value of life insurance. You are working hard to build your nest egg, so every year this is a great check to make sure you are continually adding net worth on your investment portfolio.

Anytime you are looking for help, just go to www.briandamico.com and I will make sure I make myself available to help with any questions you may have. Best Regards and Remember:

"Whenever you see a successful business, someone once made a courageous decision." ~ Peter F. Drucker

With great risk often comes great reward. There are failures, setbacks, and even complete start-overs along the way, but if you don't risk something, you'll never gain anything. Take a chance and see what rewards come out of that courageous decision.

Here's How to Take the First Step to Buying Your Own Home and Building True Wealth

You've been thinking about getting into real estate but aren't sure it's for you. You see a lot of people around the country who have made a tremendous amount of money by being a real estate owner and landlord. It's great to see all this, but you just don't know where to start.

Author Brian D'Amico came from a real estate family and he's lived through the high and low times. He owns a mortgage company called New Fed Mortgage Corp., which he started back in 2000, and has a weekly podcast called "Easy Money New England" where they like to say, "There is no such thing as Easy Money."

Brian likes to share one consistent strategy that wins no matter what the market is doing. He shares his many years of wisdom with you in an easy to understand and inspiring way. You, too, can get started on your path to real estate riches.

Hands down, real estate is the best investment you will ever make. You can see it every day—it's tangible. When you invest in stocks, you can't see it, you can't control what happens, and you never know when the next big bust is going to happen. But when you invest in real estate, you are the CEO of that property. Real estate can be a slow-moving industry, but rewarding. Home ownership has many tax advantages and allows you to create wealth without having to pay big taxes every step of the way.

Most people who just chip away at their 30-year mortgage want to be safe, with no risk. Now, as a real estate investor, you can leverage your assets and be on your way to becoming wealthy.

Sincerely,

Brian D'Amico

1-877-NewFed-1
MLO #20400
New Fed Mortgage Corp.
NMLS#1881

Made in the USA
Monee, IL
04 November 2026

67386123R10030